COME SIT AWHILE

The COMFORT of REST and REASSURANCE

INSPIRATION *from the* FRONT PORCH

by Roy Lessin & Heather Solum

BARBOUR
PUBLISHING

ISBN 1-59310-653-x

Scripture quotations marked NKJV are taken from the New King James Version. Copyright © 1979, 1980, 1982 by Thomas Nelson, Inc. Used by permission. All rights reserved.

Scripture quotations marked MSG are from *THE MESSAGE.* Copyright © by Eugene H. Peterson 1993, 1994, 1995. Used by permission of NavPress Publishing Group.

Scripture quotations marked NIV are taken from the HOLY BIBLE, NEW INTERNATIONAL VERSION®. NIV®. Copyright © 1973, 1978, 1984 by International Bible Society. Used by permission of Zondervan. All rights reserved.

Scripture quotations marked KJV are taken from the King James Version of the Bible.

Scripture quotations marked NLT are taken from the *Holy Bible,* New Living Translation, copyright © 1996. Used by permission of Tyndale House Publishers, Inc. Wheaton, Illinois 60189, U.S.A. All rights reserved.

Cover design by Greg Jackson, Jackson Design Co, llc

Cover and interior art by Barbara Pascolini

Published by Barbour Publishing, Inc., P.O. Box 719, Uhrichsville, Ohio 44683, www.barbourbooks.com

Our mission is to publish and distribute inspirational products offering exceptional value and biblical encouragement to the masses.

Member of the
Evangelical Christian
Publishers Association

Printed in China.
5 4 3 2 1

he *Come Sit Awhile* gift book series is a collection of heartwarming stories, scriptures, recipes, quotes, prayers, and inspirational thoughts of hope and encouragement. We have chosen the theme of the front porch because it not only speaks of a place where people gather, relax, and enjoy the pleasures of each other's company, but it is also symbolic of a special place in our hearts where rest is found, where we enjoy the sweetness of God's presence, and where priceless memories are gathered and cherished always.

Then Jesus said,

"Let's get away from the crowds

for a while and rest."

MARK 6:31 NLT

Your front porch may be found by
a rustic cabin that overlooks a
mountain stream; it may be a stoop
on a crowded city street; symbolically,
it may be a quiet place deep inside you. . . .
Wherever your front porch is found, it is
a place that invites you to rest, recall, and
reflect upon the things that touch you deeply,
that sweeten your life, and that draw you
closer to the heart of God.

Those who feared the LORD spoke to one another,

And the LORD listened and heard them;

So a book of remembrance was written

before Him for those who fear the LORD

and who meditate on His name.

MALACHI 3:16 NKJV

The Lord loves to listen in on the conversations of His people. He delights to hear us talking about the things that build us up and help us grow, that encourage us to trust in the promises that He has given us, that move us along in our journey, that quiet our hearts, and that affirm our faith. Most of all, He loves to hear words that are filled with thankfulness, devotion, and praise.

Ask Jesus to awaken you each morning—

so you are refreshed, renewed,

and ready to meet the day.

———————————

I will lie down and sleep in peace, for you alone,

O LORD, make me dwell in safety.

PSALM 4:8 NIV

———————————

He giveth his beloved sleep.

PSALM 127:2 KJV

DROP THY STILL DEWS
OF QUIETNESS,
TILL ALL OUR STRIVINGS CEASE;
TAKE FROM OUR SOULS
THE STRAIN AND STRESS,
AND LET OUR
ORDERED LIVES CONFESS
THE BEAUTY OF THY PEACE.

JOHN G. WHITTIER

I lie down and sleep;

I wake again,

because the LORD sustains me.

PSALM 3:5 NIV

On my bed I remember you;

I think of you

through the watches of the night.

PSALM 63:6 NIV

WE CAN CLOSE

OUR EYES KNOWING

THAT GOD HAS HIS EYE

UPON US. . . .

WE CAN SLEEP KNOWING

THAT HE IS AWAKE.

hink of yourself comfortably
stretched out on a hammock, gently rocking
under the shade of a screened-in porch.
That's the way we should be on the inside—
resting in God's care, trusting in His goodness,
leaning back in His love.

OUR GREATEST REST COMES
WHEN WE TRUST IN
THE FINISHED WORK THAT
GOD HAS DONE FOR US
THROUGH HIS SON.
IT IS A GIFT FREELY GIVEN.
IT IS NOT BASED ON
OUR PERFORMANCE,
BUT ON HIS LOVE.
HE HAS GRACIOUSLY
RELIEVED US OF THE BURDEN
OF TRYING TO SAVE OURSELVES.

Take my yoke upon you, and learn of me;

for I am meek and lowly in heart:

and ye shall find rest unto your souls.

For my yoke is easy, and my burden is light.

MATTHEW 11:29–30 KJV

esus doesn't say that He will come
and take up our yoke, but He calls us
to come and take up His. It's so good to
be joined together with Jesus in every aspect
of life, work, and devotion. His yoke will not
stress us out or burn us out. It's a yoke of
hearing His voice, sensing His peace,
learning His ways, and knowing His heart.

That Dear Front Porch

Though I've grown and changed, the front porch at my parents' house stays the same. The porch has allowed me, at any age, to be myself—some days tired and lonely, other days fresh and secure.

No matter how I enter, I always leave renewed. . . . The swing, the air, the trees, the flowers, the cars passing by, the humming of the insects—all remind me of the simplicity of relaxing. And the voices around me are the things that have meant the most. . .discussing life with those who love me. What great value and gain!

I will always hold the memories gathered from the porch at my parents' house. It has been a place of rest—from my childhood, to being held in my husband's arms, to rocking my own babies on that dear front porch.

LYDIA NAST

How excellent is thy lovingkindness, O God!

therefore the children of men put

their trust under the shadow of thy wings.

PSALM 36:7 KJV

For in the day of trouble

he will keep me safe in his dwelling.

PSALM 27:5 NIV

And we know that in all things

God works for the good of

those who love him,

who have been called

according to his purpose.

ROMANS 8:28 NIV

HAVE GREAT TRUST
IN WHAT GOD HAS PROMISED,
AND YOU WILL HAVE
GREAT CONFIDENCE
IN WHAT HE CAN DO.

Sing to the LORD *a new song,*

for he has done marvelous things;

his right hand and his holy arm

have worked salvation for him.

PSALM 98:1 NIV

GOD CAN MAKE
ALL THINGS NEW IN OUR LIVES,
JUST AS HIS MERCIES GREET US
IN A NEW WAY EVERY MORNING.
HE CAN GIVE US NEW LIFE,
A NEW HEART, NEW DESIRES,
A NEW BEGINNING,
AND A NEW SONG.

Comforting Voices

When I was a little girl, there were so many times I would beg to stay up a little longer. . .just so I could sit with the adults while they visited on our front porch. Most of the time, Mom would send me off to bed in spite of my pleas. My solace came by moving my pillow to the far end of the bed, placing my head as close as I could to the open window that was adjacent to the porch. I would lie there in the quiet of my room listening to the hum of voices that filled the night air. At times, I could hear the sweetness of Granny's voice or my mother's laughter. As my eyes grew heavy, I would drift into sleep, secure in knowing I was so close to the ones I loved and who loved me most.

LEAH KNOWLTON

Few things can create as much excitement when you're outside as the sight of a rainbow after a rain shower. The power of it, the beauty of it, the majesty of it, can take your breath away. What a glorious way for the heavens to tell us that God is faithful.

The heavens declare the glory of God;
the skies proclaim the work of his hands.

PSALM 19:1 NIV

WHEN YOU SLEEP OUTSIDE
ON A SCREENED-IN PORCH,
YOUR COMPANIONS ARE
THE SOUNDS, THE SMELLS,
AND THE WONDERS THAT
FILL A SUMMER'S NIGHT.

$\mathcal{W}$hen I married, my husband and I had a home with a front porch. In many ways, it was like the one I remembered from my grandparents' house. It was long and kind of narrow, and it had rocking chairs instead of a glider. We sat and rocked many an evening, just watching the sun go down over the foothills of the Ozark Mountains. The smell of the evening, the sounds of the crickets, and the call of the whippoorwill would bring a sense of peace at the end of the day.

The porch served us faithfully through the years. Many times, when our children and grandchildren would arrive, we would find

them all lined up on the
porch—some on the steps,
some on the railing, and
some on chairs brought out from the house.
We would talk (a porch is a wonderful place to
talk about anything), laugh, and share life with
each other. And again, we could share sunsets,
the twinkling stars of the evening, and even the
thunderstorms that would roll in over the
mountains.

In many ways, the storms were different here

than at my grandpa's. The clouds would roll over the hills, the lighting would be all around us, but the smell was the same, and I could still feel the warmth of my grandpa's arms around me and hear him saying, "This is God's way of watering the earth and providing for us."

GLORIA KNIGHT

A FRONT PORCH HAS
A UNIQUE WAY OF
BEING REASSURING;
IT ALLOWS YOU TO
SIT OUTSIDE WITH
SHELTER OVER YOUR HEAD
AND GOOD SUPPORT
UNDER YOUR FEET.

Tomorrow will bring with it nothing,

But He will bear us through;

Who gives the lilies clothing

Will clothe His people, too.

Beneath the spreading heavens

No creature but is fed;

And He who feeds the ravens

Will give His children bread.

WILLIAM COWPER

When we run a race or are very active, it is easy to become short of breath. Rest is to our inner life what air is to our lungs. The life of God is the air we breathe to revive us. When we receive God's rest, quietness comes where there once was disturbance; calm comes where there once was turmoil; and stillness comes where there once was a storm.

IN THE STRESS
AND PRESSURES OF LIFE,
GOD WANTS US TO FALL BACK
INTO HIS PROTECTIVE ARMS
OF GRACE, AND WHEN WE DO,
WE CAN BE CERTAIN THAT
HE WILL ALWAYS BE THERE
TO CATCH US.

Cast all your anxiety

on him because

he cares for you.

1 PETER 5:7 NIV

$\mathcal{I}$ love my front porch

in the cool days of autumn. . . .

I simply bundle up in an old,

warm quilt with soft cotton batting,

a book in my hands, a cup of tea by my side,

and I enter a world of restful delight!

You can have your roller-coaster rides;

I'll take the slow, easy motion

of a porch swing anytime.

There's no point restfully sitting

outside on your front porch if

you're in a hurry on the inside.

Three Things You Do Not Have to Be. . .

Do not be troubled.

JOHN 14:1

Do not be anxious.

PHILIPPIANS 4:6

Do not be afraid.

JOHN 14:27

Obedience and trust in God today is

the best preparation for tomorrow.

Let integrity and uprightness preserve me;

for I wait on thee.

PSALM 25:21 KJV

Waiting on God is not a state of panic,

but a place of rest.

———————————

Wait on the LORD: be of good courage,

and he shall strengthen thine heart:

wait, I say, on the LORD.

PSALM 27:14 KJV

When we wait on God to speak to us,

we also wait for God to work in our behalf.

When God works,

His timing is always perfect.

Rest in the LORD,

and wait patiently for him.

PSALM 37:7 KJV

You don't need to fear—

not because you are brave,

but because your heavenly Father is with you,

holding your hand.

For ye have not received

the spirit of bondage again to fear;

but ye have received the Spirit of adoption,

whereby we cry, Abba, Father.

ROMANS 8:15 KJV

But you are a shield around me,

O LORD;

you bestow glory on me

and lift up my head.

PSALM 3:3 NIV

The shield of God's presence covers you from every side. He protects you from the arrows that would stop you from moving ahead and from the arrows that fly at you from your past. When we are under spiritual attack, it is easy for our souls to become heavy and for our countenance to lose its gleam of joy. Our nights can be restless and our days covered with shadows. The deliverance that comes from God is like a gentle hand placed under our chins. . . that moves our heads upward so that our eyes can once again gaze into His face. In that gaze we see the light of His glory. . .the comfort of our Father. . .and the depth of His caring heart.

KNOW THAT THE Lord HAS

SET APART THE GODLY

FOR HIMSELF;

THE Lord WILL HEAR

WHEN I CALL TO HIM.

PSALM 4:3 NIV

There is a difference between being set aside and being set apart. God doesn't set you aside like someone who puts aside a tool he is not using. You are set apart like a diamond from common glass or an original masterpiece from a mere imitation. You are set apart from common use to holy use, from ordinary thinking to extraordinary thinking, from natural living to supernatural living, from human plans to God's purposes.

Never think of yourself as alone—

for God is with you.

Never think of yourself as defenseless—

for God is your protector.

Never think of yourself as inadequate—

for God is your provider.

Never think of yourself as useless—

for God has a purpose for your life.

Never think of yourself as hopeless—

for God has a plan for your future.

There's No One Like Jesus

To the bound, He is freedom.

To the empty, He is fullness.

To the needy, He is supply.

To the weak, He is strength.

To the sick, He is healing.

To the downcast, He is joy.

To the hurting, He is comfort.

To the defenseless, He is protection.

To the hungry, He is bread.

To the weary, He is rest.

HAVE YOU EVER LEARNED
THE BEAUTIFUL ART OF LETTING
GOD TAKE CARE OF YOU? . . .
IT WILL RELIEVE YOU
OF A THOUSAND CARES.

A. B. SIMPSON

The Lord Is Your...

Shepherd; you are cared for.

Captain; you are protected.

Encourager; you are built up.

Salvation; you are delivered.

Provider; you are blessed.

Teacher; you are instructed.

Rock; you are secure.

Victory; you are triumphant.

The Lord Is Your. . .

Healer; you are whole.

Rest; you are comforted.

Guide; you are directed.

Strength; you are able.

Father; you are accepted.

Deliverer; you are free.

Confidence; you are assured.

Maker; you are loved.

WHAT IS MEANT BY THE PEACE
THAT PASSES ALL UNDERSTANDING?
IT DOES NOT MEAN A PEACE
NO ONE CAN COMPREHEND.
IT MEANS A PEACE NO AMOUNT
OF REASONING WILL BRING. . . .
YOUR HEART CAN REST IN
PERFECT SECURITY BECAUSE
GOD KNOWS, HE LOVES, HE LEADS.

A. B. SIMPSON

By My Father's Side

In 1924, I was five years old. Our home was in Kerkhoven, Minnesota. The land was very flat there, and you could see out across the prairie for miles. The times were simple, and simple things had great meaning. One day my dad, Jonas Johnson, went out to our garden and pulled a parsnip out of the ground, peeled it, cut it into pieces, and shared this treat with me. As we sat down enjoying our treat and each other's company, I looked out into the horizon and saw a tornado move across the land. As I watched in awe, I felt no fear, for I felt safe and comforted by my father's side.

DELMA CARLSON

Whatever your trial,

God sees.

Whatever your struggle,

God knows.

Whatever your cry,

God listens.

Whatever your problem,

God understands.

Whatever your difficulty,

God cares.

EVERYTHING HE'S PROMISED
HE WILL SURELY DO—
GOD, WHO SEES THE SPARROW,
WATCHES OVER YOU.

Rest upon God with a quiet heart.

Let God take His time,

confident that God's time is better than ours.

In this age of hurry,

we need such a rest of faith.

A. C. DIXON

There is a river that begins at the heart of God;

It flows to quiet meadowlands and to where
the road is hard.

The river moves through mountains to reach
the heart of man

And nourishes it with kindness as only His
mercy can.

The river is refreshing; it washes and renews;

It brings the Spirit's presence as gently as
the dew.

The river is anointing, it's compassion and
it's grace;

The river is a healing stream and a peaceful
resting place.

There's not a promise God's ever broken;

    Nothing's failed that He has said.

He will not forsake you;

    like the sparrow you'll be fed.

God will not fail you;

    He will not leave you alone.

God will not fail you;

    He does not forsake His own.

IF OUR LIVES ARE
IN OUR OWN HANDS,
WE HAVE REASON TO WORRY;
IF OUR LIVES ARE
IN GOD'S HANDS,
WE HAVE REASON TO REST.

"*If* God cares so wonderfully for flowers

that are here today and gone tomorrow,

won't he more surely care for you?

You have so little faith!

So don't worry about having

enough food or drink or clothing."

MATTHEW 6:30–31 NLT

O the little birds sang east,

And the little birds sang west,

And I smiled to think God's greatness

Flowed around our incompleteness,

Found our restlessness, His rest.

ELIZABETH BARRETT BROWNING

The sparrow speaks;

The sound is true—

"God, your Father,

Cares for you."

"So I tell you,

don't worry about everyday life—

whether you have enough

food, drink, and clothes.

Doesn't life consist of

more than food and clothing?

Look at the birds.

They don't need to plant or harvest

or put food in barns

because your heavenly Father feeds them.

And you are far more valuable

to him than they are."

MATTHEW 6:25–26 NLT

Praise to the Lord, who o'er all things so

    wondrously reigneth,

Shelters thee under His wings, yea, so gently

    sustaineth!

Hath thou not seen, How thy desires e're

    have been

Granted in what He ordaineth?

JOACHIM NEANDER

Tribute to the Robin

I have one preacher that I love better than any other upon earth; it is my little tame robin, which preaches to me daily. I put his crumbs upon my windowsill, especially at night. He hops onto the sill when he wants his supply and takes as much as he desires to satisfy his need. From thence he always hops onto a little tree close by and lifts up his voice to God and sings his carol of praise and gratitude, tucks his little head under his wing and goes fast to sleep, and leaves tomorrow to look after itself. He is the best preacher that I have on earth.

MARTIN LUTHER

God's peace in your life

is not circumstantial, but relational.

It is not based on what

is going on around you,

but on who is living in you.

There is a treasury of reassurance found in
who God is to us—
Salvation, Redeemer, Fortress,
Deliverer, Shield, Banner,
High Tower, Righteousness,
Hiding Place,
Hope, Refuge, Peace.

When we live a life of faith in God, there are certain truths we must always come back to. When we face fear or anxiety, we must come back to the truth that God is in control; when we face hardships or disappointments, we must come back to the truth that God is good; when we face rejection or loneliness, we must come back to the truth that God is love; when we face needs or limitations, we must come back to the truth that God provides.

What then shall we say to these things?

If God is for us, who can be against us?

He who did not spare His own Son,

but delivered Him up for us all,

how shall He not with Him also

freely give us all things?

ROMANS 8:31–32 NKJV

The Front Porch Race

One story that my grandpa loved to tell me about was our race to the front porch. "When you were a little girl," he would say, "you would often look out the window to see if I was coming to visit. Whenever you saw me, you would scream out the window, race through the house, run out on the front porch as fast as you could, and jump into my arms. The moment I heard you scream, I knew I had to run as fast as I could to make sure I was there to catch you. And you know what?" he would say with a glimmer. "I never missed!"

BETTY WOMACK

BE STILL MY SOUL,

THE LORD IS ON THY SIDE.

LEAVE TO THY GOD

TO ORDER AND PROVIDE.

BE STILL MY SOUL,

THE WAVES AND WINDS STILL KNOW

HIS VOICE WHO RULED THEM

WHILE HE DWELT BELOW.

KATARINA VON SCHLEGEL

Then He arose and rebuked the wind,

and said to the sea,

"Peace, be still!"

And the wind ceased

and there was a great calm.

MARK 4:39 NKJV

Ever lift Thy face upon me,

As I work and wait for Thee;

Resting 'neath Thy smile, Lord Jesus,

Earth's dark shadows flee.

Brightness of my Father's glory,

Sunshine of my Father's face,

Keep me ever trusting, resting;

Fill me with Thy grace.

JEAN S. PIGOTT

A Prayer for Rest

Lord, calm each storm within me.

May I know Your peace,

even in the busiest times.

Move me along today at Your pace

and in Your rest.

More, and more, and more,

we need to trust Him as never before.

———————————

When I am afraid,

I will trust in you.

PSALM 56:3 NIV

YES God is guarding and guiding the desires that He has put in your heart. As you wait and rest in Him, He will work out His perfect plan for your life. Even now He is gently watching over you and protecting the work that He has begun in you. He is sheltering you and jealously keeping you from anything that would move you away from His best.

The one who calls you

is faithful

and he will do it.

1 THESSALONIANS 5:24 NIV

Moving like a mighty river,
From the heart of the life-giver
Comes a healing stream of mercy,
Living waters for the thirsty;
Washing, cleansing, and refreshing,
Bringing every heavenly blessing—
Quiet pools of peace and rest,
Giving only what is best;
Flowing from beneath the throne,
For the thirsty heart alone.

God's Peace

Peace is a guard for the words we speak.

Peace is a guide for the things we seek.

Peace is a shield for the fears we face.

Peace is a gift of amazing grace.

Delight in the Lord. . . .

    He will give you the desires of your heart.

Commit your way to the Lord and trust Him. . . .

    He will bring it to pass.

Acknowledge Him in all your ways. . . .

    He will direct your paths.

Give Him your burdens. . . .

    He will sustain you.

Obediently wait for the Lord. . . .

    He will lift you up.

LET YOUR LIFE REST IN CHRIST,

FOR HIS KINGDOM IS UNSHAKABLE.

LET YOUR CONFIDENCE

BE FIRM IN CHRIST,

FOR HIS KINGDOM IS UNMOVABLE.

LET YOUR FAITH

TRUST FULLY IN CHRIST,

FOR HIS KINGDOM IS

INDESTRUCTIBLE.

I will hear what God the LORD will speak,

For He will speak peace to His people.

PSALM 85:8 NKJV

When God leads us to do something, it may not
always be easy, but it will always be peaceful.

"Peace I leave with you,

My peace I give to you;

not as the world gives do I give to you.

Let not your heart be troubled,

neither let it be afraid."

JOHN 14:27 NKJV

When Jesus gives you something of Himself, He is giving you something that is eternal. It means that it comes to you outside any resource you have and outside any circumstance you are in. When He gives you His peace, it means that you will experience on the inside of your heart what He is experiencing inside of His.

When peace like a river attendeth my way,

When sorrows like sea billows roll,

Whatever my lot, Thou hast taught me to say,

"It is well, it is well with my soul."

HORATIO G. SPAFFORD

God has given us precious promises of peace so that we can be free of our cares, released from our burdens, delivered from our fears, and saved from our worries.

_____

Trust in him at all times.

PSALM 62:8 NIV

Give your burdens

to the LORD,

and he will take care of you.

PSALM 55.22 NLT

LORD, KEEP ME CALM
IN THE STORMS OF LIFE
AND PEACEFUL IN
THE BUSYNESS OF LIFE—
FOR YOU HAVE ASSURED ME
THAT IN QUIETNESS AND TRUST
I SHALL FIND YOUR STRENGTH.

Faith is not a wish, but a confidence;

not a dream, but a reality;

not a guess, but a certainty

that everything will turn out

exactly as God has promised.

YOU CAN HAPPILY, RESTFULLY,

CONFIDENTLY BE ANTICIPATING

EVERYTHING THAT GOD,

IN HIS LOVE,

HAS PREPARED FOR YOU.

"Eye has not seen, nor ear heard,

Nor have entered into the heart of man

The things which God has prepared

for those who love Him."

1 CORINTHIANS 2:9 NKJV

Look up to the Lord, for He will never let you down. . . .

HE SENT HIS SON
TO SAVE AND BLESS YOU.

———————

He who did not spare His own Son,

but delivered Him up for us all,

how shall He not with Him also

freely give us all things?

ROMANS 8:32 NKJV

He is faithful to His promises.

For all the promises of God in Him are Yes,

and in Him Amen,

to the glory of God through us.

2 CORINTHIANS 1:20 NKJV

*He will never
take His eyes off of you.*

I will instruct you and teach you in the way you

should go; I will guide you with My eye.

PSALM 32:8 NKJV